MEN-AT-ARMS SERIES

EDITOR: MARTIN WINDROW

Napoleon's Cuirassiers and Carabiniers

Text by   EMIR BUKHARI

Colour plates by   ANGUS McBRIDE

OSPREY PUBLISHING LIMITED

Published in 1977 by
Osprey Publishing Ltd
59 Grosvenor Street, London W1X 9DA
© Copyright 1977 Osprey Publishing Ltd
Reprinted 1978, 1980, 1981, 1983, 1984, 1985 (twice),
1987, 1988, 1989

The author would like to express his gratitude
for the assistance rendered him by the following
persons in the preparation of this book: the staffs
of the Musée de l'Armée, Paris, and the National
Army Museum, London; Michel Risser; Jean de
Gerlache; Blaise Morgan (photographer); and Sue A.
and Mary P. The author would also like to acknowledge
the debt owed to Lucien Rousselot by all writers and
illustrators concerned with the French Army. Without his research foreign-language works on this
period would be the poorer. The line illustrations in
this book were drawn after his diagrams.

ISBN 0 85045 096 9

Filmset by BAS Printers Limited, Wallop, Hampshire
Printed in Hong Kong

Organisation

The entire French army was reorganised in 1791, and all old regimental titles were abolished. Regiments were once more commanded by colonels and included the following officers: two lieutenant-colonels, a *quartier-maître trésorier* (paymaster quartermaster), a surgeon major, a chaplain, two adjutants, a trumpet-major and five *maîtres-ouvriers*. The two regiments of carabiniers were composed of four squadrons each and the 27 *cavalerie* regiments of three squadrons, each of two companies which included: a captain, a lieutenant, two second-lieutenants, a *maréchal-des-logis-chef*, two *maréchaux-des-logis*, a *brigadier-fourrier*, four *brigadiers*, 54 troopers and a trumpeter. In 1792, the *cavalerie* regiments were reduced to 25 and, in 1793, had the number of squadrons brought up to four. Also in 1793 colonels were renamed as *chefs de brigade* and lieutenant-colonels as *chefs d'escadron*.

Upon becoming First Consul, Bonaparte restored the title of colonel and introduced that of major. In September of that same year, 1802, he wrote to General Berthier, Minister of War: 'I desire you, citizen minister, to submit to me a scheme for reducing the regiments of heavy cavalry to twenty – two of which should be carabiniers – all four squadrons strong. The last six of the now existing regiments should be broken up to furnish a squadron to each of the first eighteen proposed regiments. Of the eighteen regiments, the first five are to wear the cuirass, in addition to the eighth, which is already equipped in this manner, making in all, six regiments with, and twelve regiments without cuirasses'. The 1st regiment of *cavalerie* had, on 10 October 1801, already been converted to the 1st Cavalerie-Cuirassiers and, on 12 October 1802, the 2nd, 3rd and 4th regiments

followed suit; shortly thereafter, on 23 December 1802, the 5th, 6th and 7th did likewise. Within a year the 9th, 10th, 11th and 12th regiments were also transformed, bringing the new arm to a strength of twelve cuirassier regiments. This situation remained static until, in 1808, the 1st Pro-

A trooper of the 12th Cuirassiers, October 1804. Formed in late 1803, this regiment remained without cuirasses until 1804. Although issued with a short-tailed tunic from 1803, the cuirassiers were obliged to continue wearing their cumbersome long-tailed *cavalerie* tunics until they wore out; this particular *habit-veste* is interesting in that it is of 1803 cut but complete with lapels, of which the 1803 pattern was devoid. Reconstructed after an inspection report, it demonstrates how frequently the reality of uniform differed from the official orders. The 5th Cuirassiers are also reported as having had lapels of the regimental colour. Just visible is the single-section *cavalerie* swordbelt which was found to hold the sabre too high for an armoured horseman and was duly replaced by the 'AnXI' pattern of three sections, which suspended the sabre at wrist height. The sabre is the 'AnIX' model soon to be replaced by the guttered 'AnXI' pattern (**Illustration by L. Rousselot, courtesy of the De Gerlache de Gomery Collection**)

Left:
A squadron of heavy cavalry in column by fours. In this formation, a regiment seen from above would have the 1st and 3rd squadrons abreast, followed by the 2nd and 4th squadrons, reading from left to right. Where each trooper occupied a metre in width, the length of a squadron in column by fours would be approximately 80m., excluding the officer and NCOs at each extremity. Squadrons would follow one another at a distance of around 13 m.
Key: C = captain. L = lieutenant. Sl = sous-lieutenant. Mc = maréchal-des-logis-chef. M = maréchal-des-logis. Bf = brigadier-fourrier. B = brigadier

Above:
The first squadron of a heavy cavalry regiment in column by troop preceded by the regiment's trumpets. In column by troop, a squadron would have a frontage of 12m. exclusive of officers and NCOs extending beyond the limit of the second rank. The troops would maintain a distance of 12m. between each other, measured from nose to nose of the horses, that they might swing into line, facing in either direction, should necessity arise. Squadrons would ride 24m. behind one another
Key: A = adjutant. Am = adjutant-major. C = captain. L = lieutenant. Sl = sous-lieutenant. Mc = maréchal-des-logis-chef. M = maréchal-des-logis. Bf = brigadier-fourrier. B = brigadier

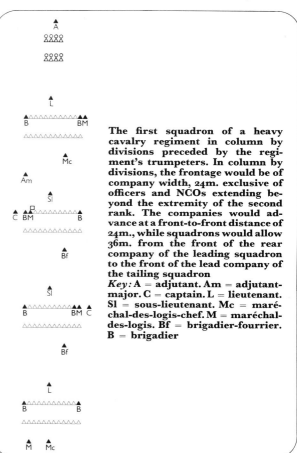

visional Regiment of Heavy Cavalry became the 13th Cuirassiers, followed by the 2nd regiment of Dutch cuirassiers who, in 1810, were renamed the 14th Cuirassiers.

As we have seen, the regiments were composed of four squadrons, raised to five in March of 1807, each of two companies of two troops apiece. In 1806 the regimental staff in theory consisted of a colonel, a major, two *chefs d'escadron*, two *adjutant-majors*, a paymaster-quartermaster, a surgeon-major, an *aide-major*, two *sous-aide-major*, two

The first squadron of a heavy cavalry regiment in column by divisions preceded by the regiment's trumpeters. In column by divisions, the frontage would be of company width, 24m. exclusive of officers and NCOs extending beyond the extremity of the second rank. The companies would advance at a front-to-front distance of 24m., while squadrons would allow 36m. from the front of the rear company of the leading squadron to the front of the lead company of the tailing squadron
Key: A = adjutant. Am = adjutant-major. C = captain. L = lieutenant. Sl = sous-lieutenant. Mc = maréchal-des-logis-chef. M = maréchal-des-logis. Bf = brigadier-fourrier. B = brigadier

adjutants, a *brigadier-trompette*, a veterinary surgeon and six *maîtres* (i.e. cobblers, tailors, armourers and saddlers).

Each company supposedly boasted a captain, a lieutenant, a second-lieutenant, a *maréchal-des-logis-chef*, four *maréchaux-des-logis*, a *fourrier*, eight *brigadiers*, 82 troopers and a trumpeter. That this was the exception and not the rule is certain. Consider the following returns of the two divisions of heavy cavalry in the reserve cavalry corps of the

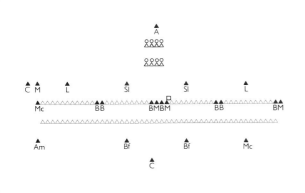

The first squadron of a heavy cavalry regiment in formation of *colonne serré* preceded by the regiment's trumpeters. The *colonne serré* comprised of the squadrons extended to total length, 48m. exclusive of officers and NCOs extending beyond the extremity of the second row, and formed up one behind the other at a distance of 16m. from the front of the lead squadron to the front of the following squadron. The total depth of such a formation would be 54m., excluding officers, NCOs and trumpeters

Key: **A** = adjutant. **Am** = adjutant-major. **C** = captain. **L** = lieutenant. **Sl** = sous-lieutenant. **Mc** = maréchal-des-logis-chef. **M** = maréchal-des-logis. **Bf** = brigadier-fourrier. **B** = brigadier

Grande Armée of 1805:

Nansouty's First Division:	Officers	Men	Horses
2nd Cuirassiers	22	510	469
9th Cuirassiers	22	491	513
3rd Cuirassiers	20	500	475
12th Cuirassiers	24	566	590
D'Hautpoul's Second Division:			
1st Cuirassiers	32	498	500
5th Cuirassiers	32	468	367
10th Cuirassiers	32	551	475
11th Cuirassiers	32	539	443

Official policy and reality should never be confused; and this should be borne in mind when considering the dress and equipment of the heavy cavalry, the subject of the next section.

Dress and Equipment

As we have all too briefly noted, the cuirassiers and carabiniers had something of a common history and this was reflected in their dress. It was only after the Austrian campaign of 1809 that any great fundamental change was wrought and, paradoxically, this in many ways accentuated their resemblance.

Owing to the heavy casualties suffered by the carabiniers in the 1809 campaign, the Emperor determined to protect these élite cavalrymen better and, in an edict dated 24 December 1809, he decreed that they should be armoured to the same advantage as the cuirassiers while still maintaining their separate identity. This last was provided by changing the basic colour of their uniforms from dark blue to white which contrasted bril-

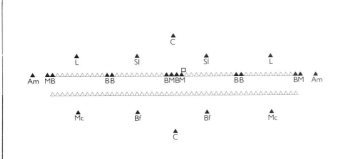

A squadron of heavy cavalry drawn up in battle order. Battle order, like the *colonne serré*, involved the squadron presenting its full double-row length of 48m., excluding officers and NCOs beyond the extremities of the second rank. A regiment so developed could either have all its squadrons in line, running from 1st to 4th from right to left, or one behind the other with 9m. between the back of the leading squadron and the front of the trailing one, reading 1st, 3rd, 4th and 2nd from the front backwards

Key: **A** = adjutant. **Am** = adjutant-major. **C** = captain. **L** = lieutenant. **Sl** = sous-lieutenant. **Mc** = maréchal-des-logis-chef. **M** = maréchal-des-logis. **Bf** = brigadier-fourrier. **B** = brigadier

A trooper of the 5th Cuirassiers in campaign dress, post 1812. Here, a little removed from the pomp of the paradeground, this trooper has made several concessions to the realities of the march: his tall scarlet plume has been encased in an oilskin envelope and left atop the helmet; and the long horse-hair mane of the helmet has been plaited along its entire length (designed to control it in high winds or devised to dispel the boredom of irksome guard-duty?) He carries a spare pair of boots strapped to the top of his portemanteau, suggesting that he is either very fortunate or has just left a rather unfortunate comrade lying in the grass; he wears linen overalls over his hide breeches to protect them from the elements; and, finally, has tied his horse's tail into a knot to avoid it becoming tangled in the undergrowth (*Illustration by Job, courtesy of the National Army Museum*)

liantly with the copper-plated armour with which they were issued. In this way the two corps drew together in being the only troops of the Grande Armée who were armoured, while at the same time they diverged in breaking away from their traditionally similar dress.

ARMOUR

Headgear

The cuirassier helmet consisted of an iron cap surrounded by a fur turban and with a copper crest surmounted by a horsehair mane. Helmets differed, however, in points of detail, for each

regiment purchased its own: thus the height of the cap, the shape of the peak, the degree of curve and type of ornament of the crest, and the socket of the horsehair aigrette varied considerably. In 1811, an attempt was made to rationalise the situation by producing a universal pattern. Unfortunately, from an urge to simplify grew a desire to economise and the new model was far from popular owing to its shoddy manufacture: the low quality of the iron, copper and horsehair, the absence of a metal edge to the peak which resulted in its losing shape, and the removal of the heavy embossing which had given the crest its solidity, made it a poor substitute for the old patterns. Indeed, the troops were so unhappy with them that many retained their old helmets, patching them up as best they could, trusting to their greater strength. Despite protest, the helmet continued to be issued without modification to the chagrin of all: '. . . [the helmet] thought to be so good in principle is so defective that we ought to hasten to replace almost all those currently in use,' lamented General Saint-Germain in 1814.

Cuirassier officers' helmets were essentially the same although of better quality. There was, however, a more marked and distinctive evolution of shape in their patterns: while at first very similar to the troopers', around 1808 a subtle change became apparent in the angle of inclination of the crest towards the front and the degree to which the increasingly high dome of the cap slouched towards the rear; this was the first step towards the so-called 'Minerva-style' helmet with its neo-Grecian profile. This change was not born out of any desire to emulate classical elegance, but rather from a vain craving to look as smart as the armoured dragoons of the Imperial Guard.

Both officers and men sported a plume inserted in a holder just forward of the left-hand chinstrap rose. These were scarlet, except those worn by senior officers and staff, which were white.

Musicians' helmets were identical with those of the men excepting for a white horsehair mane, an occasional scarlet aigrette and the use of a non-scarlet plume. Here are a few recorded plume colours:

1st Cuirassiers   – white tipped scarlet, 1805–10 (after Wurtz).

    – white, 1811 (after Col. Jolly).

2nd Cuirassiers	–	white with scarlet tip and base, 1804–7 (after Marckolsheim).
5th Cuirassiers	–	scarlet tipped white, 1808 (after Marckolsheim).
7th Cuirassiers	–	yellow, 1810 (after Martinet).
9th Cuirassiers	–	white, 1804–5 (after Marckolsheim).
	–	black tipped yellow, 1805–6 (after Marckolsheim).
10th Cuirassiers	–	pink, 1811 (after de Ridder).
	–	yellow with white base, 1810
	–	(after Marckolsheim).
	–	scarlet tipped white, 1809 (after Marckolsheim).
13th Cuirassiers	–	scarlet tipped white, 1810 (after Marckolsheim).
14th Cuirassiers	–	scarlet with white base, 1810 (after Suhr).

The carabiniers' helmet was of yellow copper with iron chinstrap scales and roses, and headband. The crest had a scarlet comb in place of a mane. The officers' version was similar but made of red copper and silver, where a trooper's would be yellow copper and iron; further, the crest was much more extensively embossed and boasted a more voluminous scarlet comb.

The trumpeters wore troopers' helmets, complete with scarlet (in accordance with the 1812 Regulations) or light blue combs.

Cuirasses

The 'MkI cuirass' dated back to 1802 and was that year issued to the 1st Cuirassiers. The following year the 2nd, 3rd, 6th, 7th and 8th Cuirassiers were given theirs, while the 4th, 9th, 10th, 11th and 12th Cuirassiers waited until 1804 and the 5th Cuirassiers until 1805 to be armoured. The breastplate of this model was not very rounded and formed a blunt angle at the bottom; a total of 34 copper rivets were driven into the perimeters of both breast and back plate. The cuirass was put on by first hooking the ends of the metal-scaled, cloth-covered, leather shoulder straps to the spherical copper buttons riveted to the breastplate, lifting the ensemble over the head, then fastening the two halves together at the waist by means of a copper-buckled leather belt which was secured to

the back plate by twin copper rivets at each end. Though shoulder straps were normally covered in brass scales, those of the 9th Cuirassiers were armoured with twin yellow-copper chains along their length, and those of the 8th Cuirassiers were devoid of any metal, being merely unadorned black leather.

After 1806, a 'MkII cuirass' came to be issued but it differed from the 'MkI' only in that the bottom of the breastplate had been rounded-off. As of 1809 the 'MkIII cuirass' made its appearance, differing only in having a more rounded profile and being slightly shorter.

The officers' pattern of the 'MkI cuirass' was more stylish; a deeply engraved single line, placed 3cm from the edge, described a margin about the perimeter of the breast and back plates into which 32 gilded copper rivets were driven. Though at first resembling those of the men but with gilded scales and silver lace down their lengths, the shoulder straps of the officers later tended to be armoured with two or three lengths of gilded chain. The officers' waistbelt was of red leather, embroidered with silver thread and secured by means of a gilded buckle. Their 'MkII' and 'MkIII' pattern cuirasses were only slightly modified versions of the 'MkI', becoming rounder, longer and heavier, and acquiring 34 gilded rivets.

The carabiniers' iron cuirass was covered overall by a thin sheet of brass which left but a 25mm.- margin of white metal about the edge, into which the yellow copper rivets were inserted. The cuirass was otherwise essentially no different from the cuirassier version save for the natural leather waistbelt and shoulder straps, both of which had copper fittings.

The carabinier officers' model was very distinctive, with a red copper 'skin' in place of brass, a silver sunburst at the centre of the breast, light blue silver-edged cloth on the shoulder straps, and a light blue waistbelt embroidered with silver thread and secured by a silver buckle. Where the troopers' visible lining was edged in white lace, subalterns adopted twin rows of silver lace while superior officers enjoyed the privilege of a silver laurel leaf repeat-pattern embroidered directly on to the dark blue cloth.

TUNICS

The Cuirassiers

The 1803 habit-surtout: The inconvenient, long-tailed habit worn by the *cavalerie* was, by order of the *Ier Vendémiaire An XII*, to be replaced by a single-breasted, shorter-skirted *habit-surtout* provided from the funds of each individual regiment. The facing colours and their disposition were to remain the same as under the 1791 regulations, that is:

TABLE OF FACING COLOURS, 1791-1810

Facing colour				Position
Scarlet	Jonquil			
1	4	7	10	Collar, cuffs, cuff-flaps and turn-backs
2	5	8	11	Cuffs and turnbacks
3	6	9	12	Collar, cuff-flaps and turnbacks
H	V	H	V	
(Direction of pockets)				

Where the facings remained dark blue, they would be piped in the regimental colour and *vice versa* where the facings were of the regimental colour. The simulated tail pockets were contrived with piping of the distinctive colour and three pewter buttons stamped with the regimental number.

A letter dated 20 September 1803 from the War Ministry to the administrative board of the 9th Cuirassiers informs us that the *habit-surtout* was to have had shoulder-straps of dark blue, piped in the regimental colour, and to have been devoid of emblem on the turnbacks. We can be sure, however, that by this date all regiments had adopted all the symbols of élite status: plumes and epaulettes of scarlet, and dark blue grenade devices on the turnbacks.

Dismounted cuirassiers in Hamburg, 1813. These dismounted cuirassiers wear the updated *habit-veste* specified by the 1812 Regulations, with its waist-fastening, lapelled breast and short skirt. On the right is a trumpeter dressed in the Imperial Livery of 1811 with the unusual, for this date, headdress of a colpack. The figure on the far left is wearing black gaiters, a more usual form of legwear for foot duty than the heavy riding boots of his comrades (*Illustration by Job, courtesy of the National Army Museum*)

The 1806 habit-veste: Though the 1803 *habit-surtout* was worn throughout the Bavarian campaign, it would seem that the Prussian and Polish campaigns of 1806 and 1807 saw the use of an identical tunic embellished with lapels of the regimental colour. There would seem to be no logical or practical reason for the readoption of squared lapels and we must assume the motivation to have been to render the *habit-surtout* more French in appearance or simply more colourful when worn without the cuirass.

The 1809 habit-surtout: In 1809, a new *habit-surtout* was devised which differed considerably from the 1803 pattern: the tunic had ten pewter buttons in a single row down the breast and mid thigh-length tails without pockets or turnbacks. This garment immediately presented problems for, without pockets, the 1st and 4th, 2nd and 5th, 3rd and 6th, 7th and 10th, 8th and 11th, and 9th and 12th regiments were seemingly indistinguishable. As a consequence, late in 1810, a new system of facing colours was devised on the following lines:

TABLE OF FACING COLOURS, 1810-1812

Facing colour				Position
Scarlet	Aurore	Jonquil	Pink	
1	4	7	10	Collar and cuffs
2	5	8	11	Cuffs only
3	6	9	12	Collar only

Until late 1810, therefore, we can only assume that the regiments took on the above colours unofficially, sewed on directional pocket piping, attached a colour patch to the collar of the tunics or, simply, were unrecognisable except by the stamped number on their buttons.

At this stage, two new regiments were created, the 13th and 14th Cuirassiers, and they were assigned the facing colour of *lie de vin*. The 13th regiment displayed the colour on collar and cuffs while the 14th carried it only on the cuffs.

The 1812 habit-veste: As early as 1810, much criticism had been levelled at the 1809 *habit-surtout* on account of the length of the tails which, though shorter than those of the old *cavalerie* habits, were still so long as to be rucked up by the cuirass and come between trooper and saddle. A new pattern of *habit-veste* was therefore designed, single-breasted with nine pewter buttons and very short-skirted, with turnbacks and vertical simulated pockets. The regimental colour was used on the collars and turnbacks of all regiments, leaving the problem of identification to the cuffs and cuff-flaps as shown in the table below:

TABLE OF FACING COLOURS, 1812–1815

	Facing colour			Position
Scarlet	Aurore	Jonquil	Pink	
1	4	7	10	Cuffs and cuff-flaps
2	5	8	11	Cuffs only
3	6	9	12	Cuff-flaps only

This garment marked the last change in the development of a suitable tunic for troops wearing a cuirass and it was worn throughout the rest of the reported period.

A brief note on the dress of officers would not be out of place. Although they wore tunics basically identical with those of the troopers, with the exception of silver buttons, grenade patches and epaulette loops, there was a considerable latitude in dress which bears examination. In day-to-day wear the officers favoured the old *cavalerie* habit, with its long skirt and coloured lapels; having retained this garment, they took to wearing it again in service dress in 1806, when the troopers acquired their short-skirted lapelled *habit-vestes*. With the introduction of the 1809 *habit-surtout*, the *cavalerie* habit resumed its place in purely everyday wear alongside a *surtout* tunic identical with the *habit-surtout* but without piping down the breast. The 1812 Regulations prescribed a dark blue undress *surtout* with scarlet turnbacks and piping, edging collar, cuffs and breast; but they also specified that a long-tailed habit was to be worn in society and this garment was undoubtedly a modernised *cavalerie* habit, identical but for the fact that it was cut slimmer and fastened to the waist.

The Carabiniers

The 1791 habit-veste: Prior to 1810, the carabiniers wore a modernised *cavalerie habit-veste* of dark blue with scarlet lapels, cuffs and turnbacks

piped in dark blue, and dark blue collar piped in scarlet. The two regiments were distinguished solely by the cuff-flaps which were scarlet piped in dark blue for the 1st regiment, and dark blue piped in scarlet for the 2nd. Interestingly, Martinet depicts troops of the first regiment wearing tunics with scarlet collars: could this have been an attempt to identify each regiment more readily? If so, it was unofficial and certainly of very short duration. The *habit-veste* had scarlet epaulettes, edged in white lace, pewter buttons and, prior to 1809, dark blue grenade devices on the turnbacks; as of 1809, these last were white.

The 1805 surtout: A single-breasted *surtout* tunic was more frequently worn on service than the habit. Save for the scarlet turnbacks, the garment was entirely dark blue with scarlet piping about the collar, cuffs and down the breast. Between six and eight pewter buttons ran down the front, while two were worn in the small of the back, one was sewn on each shoulder and a pair were worn on each cuff.

The 1810 habit-veste: The white, single-breasted *habit-veste* issued at the time the carabiniers were armoured was of the same pattern as that worn by the cuirassiers after 1812. The collar, cuffs and turnbacks were light blue, piped in white, and light blue piping ornamented the breast and contoured the false pockets of the skirt. Again, the regiments were identified by the cuff-flaps: those of the 1st regiment were white piped in light blue and those of the 2nd were the reverse; this situation was altered only slightly in 1812, when the 1st regiment was given scarlet cuffs in place of light blue.

Officers wore basically the same pattern of *habit-veste* as the men, both before and after 1810,

but made of finer cloth and with silver buttons, epaulette loops and grenade devices. After 1810, they were issued with a new long-tailed *surtout* of light blue with white piping down the breast and about the collar and cuffs; the turnbacks were white with silver grenades. The 1812 Regulations specified the turnbacks to be henceforth light blue but it is extremely unlikely that this was ever brought about. For ball dress, a long-tailed white *surtout* with facings and ornaments identical to the *habit-veste* was worn.

LEGWEAR

The Cuirassiers
The sheep or deer-hide breeches of the cuirassiers were reserved for parade dress and, on the march and when campaigning, they would be replaced by overalls. No official mention of these exists prior to 1812. They were manufactured of linen or hide varying in colour from light grey through grey-brown, sometimes with and sometimes without cloth-covered or bone buttons down the outer seams, for lack of official prescription. For town or society dress, linen breeches and stockings or gaiters were worn; these would be white in summer and dark blue, with dark blue or black woollen stockings, in winter. The 1812 Regulations made no adjustment to town dress but did describe an official pattern of overalls: grey linen with cloth-covered buttons down the length of the outer seams.

Officers' breeches were of deer or chamois-hide, but these too would be replaced on active service with dark blue linen ones. Officers' society dress would include white linen breeches and white cotton stockings in summer, and dark blue linen or cashmere breeches with dark blue or black woollen stockings in winter.

The Carabiniers
Before 1810, the carabiniers wore sheep's-hide breeches under overalls of dark blue linen or unbleached cloth; this last variety would have twelve bone buttons down the outer seam of each leg. After 1810, linen overalls of grey-brown with buttons down the leg were used, conforming to the pattern later set out in the 1812 Regulations. White

A trumpeter of carabiniers, 1812. There were eight such trumpeters per regiment, one for every company. Between 1810 and 1812 the trumpeters wore a sky blue tunic with white lace, but from 1812 they adopted the Imperial Livery along with the rest of the musicians of the line; in their case with sky blue collar and turnbacks, and cuffs of scarlet, for the 1st regiment, and sky blue for the 2nd. The trumpet banner illustrated here is of the 1812 pattern, but it is highly unlikely that these expensive items were ever manufactured (*Illustration by Job, courtesy of the National Army Museum*)

linen breeches, replaced prior to 1810 with dark blue pairs in winter, were worn in town dress with white cotton stockings in summer and dark blue or black stockings in winter.

The officers wore deer-hide breeches beneath dark blue or unbleached cloth overalls in the same manner as the men. Similarly, in society dress, white linen or cashmere breeches and white cotton stockings were carried in summer and, before 1810, dark blue or black breeches and black stockings in winter.

COATS AND CAPES

The Cuirassiers
The cuirassiers at first received a three quarter-length, sleeveless cape with a short shoulder cape attached, made of white mixed with a dash of blue cloth. The insides of the front opening and the back vent of this rather shapeless cloak were edged with serge of the regimental colour. The 1812 Regulations ordered the manufacture of a slimmer, sleeved version of the cape, giving it the smarter appearance of a greatcoat. In 1813 a small modification was made in the removal of the coloured serge from the interior edges of the front and back openings.

The officers' patterns of the troopers' capes were identical save that they were in finer cloth and dark blue in colour. Officers also wore a dark blue overcoat which reached to approximately mid calf; this garment was double-breasted, seven silver buttons to the row, and had a large fold-down collar.

The Carabiniers
The carabiniers' capes were the same as those of the cuirassiers except for the serge lining: at first scarlet, it then became sky blue in 1810, only to be dropped altogether the following year; with the advent of the sleeved cape, the sky blue lining was

Officer of the 6th Cuirassiers in full dress, 1807. This dashing fellow is either a rich staff officer or a superior officer of some means, since only they wore white rather than scarlet plumes, and such a saddle was certainly not regulation issue. The leopard-skin shabraque, covering a natural leather French or English saddle, has a scarlet fringe and silver lace edging. It is a little unlikely that even the most flamboyant dandy – and the cuirassiers boasted not a few – would go into battle so dressed and accoutred, and we might more readily expect to meet this character at a full-dress parade (*Illustration by Benigni after Vernet, courtesy of the De Gerlache de Gomery Collection*)

A trooper of the 13th Cuirassiers, 1811–13. The 13th Cuirassiers were formed in 1808 from the *1er Régiment Provisoire de Grosse Cavalerie* and saw lengthy service in the Peninsula. It was there that this fellow acquired his brown trousers, manufactured, like so many overalls and jackets in this theatre of war, of confiscated monks' habit fabric. Of further interest is his black gourde, strung on a light blue cord; his striped swordknot, contrived from a fragment of rag; and the net of fodder attached to his saddle, a vital reserve in so inhospitable a land (*Illustration by Benigni, courtesy of the De Gerlache de Gomery Collection*)

resurrected, but removed again in 1813.

Prior to 1810, officers wore capes and overcoats of precisely the same colour and pattern as those of cuirassier officers, with the addition of a strip of silver lace to the short shoulder cape of the three quarter-length cape. After 1810 a sky blue sleeved cape, again with silver lace about the shoulder cape, was adopted, essentially no different from the model worn by the men. A sky blue overcoat was also sported, of identical cut to that worn previously.

WEAPONS

Sabres

From 1803 through 1805 the cuirassiers were issued with the flat and straight-edged 'An IX'

pattern sabre with a plain iron scabbard. At this period the regulation swordbelt was of the old *cavalerie* design, as worn by carabiniers prior to 1810, which held the sabre at an angle at waist height; this was a rather impractical arrangement for armoured troops since the cuirass impeded the drawing of the sword and emitted an unmilitary 'clang' at the least movement of the wearer. The situation was resolved by the adoption of the 'An XI' pattern waistbelt which suspended the sabre from a pair of slings, the hilt at wrist level. This improvement was soon followed by the distribution of the 'An XI' pattern sabre with its 97cm. twin-guttered blade and more robust iron scabbard. The standing height of this sword, sheathed, was 120cm.

Cuirassier officers were armed with a '*sabre de bataille*' with either a straight or lightly curved blued steel blade engraved along a third of its length. Both types of sabre fitted into the same variety of scabbard and these were either of black leather with gilded copper fittings or of browned sheet iron reinforced with gilded copper. The sabre was at first carried in a three-section sword-belt much like the troopers' 'An XI' model, but as the years wore on a slimmer single-section belt tended to be favoured; both varieties were secured with a gilded copper buckle bearing a grenade emblem. For town and society dress, officers carried a short épée in a waistbelt.

Before 1810, the carabiniers were issued either the 'An IV' or 'An IX' pattern sabre. The 'An IV' model stood 115cm. tall when sheathed and had a copper guard with a grenade device stamped upon it; the blade was straight and flat and the scabbard was of black leather with brass fittings. The 'An XI' pattern differed only in that the guard had an additional branch and the scabbard fittings were of red copper. These were sheathed at first in the

Carabiniers in full dress, 1812–15. As of 1810, the carabiniers were armoured and clothed in a new uniform of white. A difficulty with this costume was the fact that since the two regiments were only distinguishable by the colour of their cuffs, identification problems arose when the troops wore gloves; this was never resolved. Although here cylindrical, portemanteaux could equally well be rectangular. The chevrons on the left upper arms of three of the figures denote periods of service, each one presented after the individual had completed between eight and ten years under arms (Illustration by Job, courtesy of the National Army Museum)

1801 pattern single-section swordbelt which had the frog suspended at an angle by two straps sewn directly to the belt. This was replaced by the three-section 'An XI' pattern which hung the frog from the two copper rings which linked the belt together. In both cases, the bayonet frog was sewn directly to the belt at a perpendicular angle and the belt fastened by a brass buckle with grenade device. A peculiarity of carabiniers of this period was their black leather swordknot with scarlet tassel: although all mounted troops were strictly required to have swordknots through which to slip their hands before drawing their sabres, carabiniers were the only ones accorded the privilege of black leather straps in place of cloth.

Upon becoming armoured in 1810, the cara-

Troopers of the 13th Cuirassiers, 1812. These battle-weary veterans are dressed for the long haul back to France from the Peninsula. In their bundle and portemanteau are either the tattered remains of their habits or a few souvenirs of the hospitality of the pillaged churches and monasteries they leave behind. They are wearing the equivalent of stable dress, comprising a dark blue shell jacket and fatigue cap. The trousers and sandals were no doubt acquired while on campaign, for lack of supplies of regulation issue (*Illustration by Benigni, courtesy of the De Gerlache de Gomery Collection*)

A chef d'escadron of the 5th Cuirassiers in service dress, 1812. This officer wears regulation dress for the march: a helmet without plume and dark blue breeches in place of those of deer- or chamois-hide. His saddle is also of regulation pattern, though a half-shabraque of black sheepskin with 'wolves' teeth' edging of the regimental colour was more frequently employed than the cloth holster covers seen here. Note that the tail of his horse has been clubbed (*Illustration by Benigni, after Adam, courtesy of the De Gerlache de Gomery Collection*)

biniers were obliged to acquire sabres with a curved blade '*à la Montmorency*'. While awaiting these however, they retained their old straight sabres but housed them in the iron 'An XI' dragoon pattern scabbards. It would seem that the carabiniers were rather attached to their old sabres with the prestigious grenade symbol upon the guard and, having received the Montmorency blades, they had the hilts soldered to the new sabre rather than loose them. The dragoon pattern scabbards were now discarded and replaced by either a curved iron or a black leather version, with copper fittings. The distinctive black leather swordknots also had to go and these were exchanged for white buff models with scarlet tassels.

Carabinier officers also carried a sabre with a grenade device on the guard; the hilt would be

brass, red copper or gilded copper and the blade straight or lightly curved. It appears that after 1810 officers still carried a straight-bladed sabre if they so chose. The scabbards would be of black leather with gilded copper fittings, and the swordknots were gold. Like cuirassier officers, officers of carabiniers at first wore a three-section swordbelt but later opted for the single-section variety.

FIREARMS

Despite the official directive to arm the cuirassiers with muskets looted from the Vienna arsenal in 1805, they were only equipped with pistols until 1812. The pistols issued were of the 'An IX' and 'An XIII' patterns of which the 'An XIII' model had the following characteristics: *total length*, 35·2cm.; *length of barrel*, 20·7cm.; *weight*,

1·269kg.; *calibre*, 17·1mm. Most contemporary illustrations therefore show cuirassiers without cartridge-pouches, and indeed inspection reports for 1805 and 1807 list the following regiments as having none: the 3rd, 4th, 7th and 8th regiments in 1805, and the 4th, 6th, 7th and 8th regiments in 1807; just what the 6th Cuirassiers did with theirs during 1806 I leave to the reader's imagination. For those troops who were equipped with a cartridge-pouch, it would conform to the 1801 pattern and be of black leather with a buff button-holed strap by which to secure it from flapping about by fastening it to a tunic button.

Further to the Imperial Decree of 24 December 1811, the cuirassiers were equipped with the 'An XI' pattern cavalry musketoon complete with crossbelt and bayonet, in early 1812. The musketoon was approximately 115cm. long with an 85cm. barrel and the bayonet, sheathed in a scabbard inserted in a frog sewn to the middle section of the swordbelt, had a blade 46cm. long. The musketoon was slung on a crossbelt, thrown over the left shoulder and fixed to the cartridge-pouch belt by means of a spherical button. It incorporated a steel clip, through which a ring on the left side of the musketoon was passed, and a buff strap, which was wound once about the lock and then buckled. The cartridge-pouch was of the 1812 pattern, 23cm. by 14cm., and of black leather with the securing strap now moved to the top and with the addition of two buff straps beneath it for carrying the rolled-up fatigue-cap. Neither officers or musicians were armed with muskets, consequently neither carried cartridge-pouches.

The carabiniers not only carried the 'An IX' and 'An XIII' pistols but were additionally armed with muskets. Contemporary illustrations depict carabiniers with long and short muskets and, for lack of any official information, we can only hazard that these are probably the 'An IX' and 'An XIII' dragoon patterns, standing at 1·463m. and 1·415m. respectively, and the 'An IX' artillery pattern at 1·305m. The bayonet was hung in a frog stitched to the swordbelt but, unlike the sabre, at the perpendicular. The cartridge-pouch in use prior to 1812 was of black leather, approximately 24cm. by 16cm., with a brass grenade badge and a strap by which to secure it to a button on the tunic.

Early in 1812, the carabiniers were also issued the 'An IX' cavalry musketoon and bayonet complete with cartridge-pouch and musket crossbelt. Note however that these were no idle replacement for their old muskets and equipment, since these had been surrendered with their old uniforms in 1810. Like the cuirassiers, the officers and musicians of carabiniers were not equipped with muskets or musketoons and therefore did not wear a cartridge-pouch.

SADDLES AND HARNESS

The Consulate decree of 26 October 1801 (*4 Brumaire An X*) fixed the basic colour of *cavalerie* regiments' saddles as dark blue edged in white lace, and so it was to remain for cuirassiers throughout the Empire period, and for carabiniers' until 1810.

Dismounted cuirassiers, 1812. The Russian campaign was a nightmare for the cavalry; at Borodino, no less than 6,000 horses were killed, but many thousands more died through malnutrition and lack of veterinary care. After only 20km. of the retreat from Moscow, the cuirassiers were obliged to walk their starving mounts and, within five days of the first snow, the staggering loss of 30,000 horses had been reached. Following this campaign, the 1st Cuirassiers, to a man, found themselves serving on foot (*Illustration by Benigni, after Guesse, courtesy of the De Gerlache de Gomery Collection*)

The sabre in action. This ink drawing demonstrates firstly the manner in which the sabre was wielded in the charge, and, secondly, what became of the well-dressed lines once the charge got under way. The heavy cavalry sabre was a thrust weapon and, though sharp of edge, was never used to cut; the troopers therefore leaned well forward in the saddle, right arm thrust out as far as it would stretch with sabre continuing the plunge towards the enemy; in this illustration, the troopers' elbows are bent to a rather marked degree whereas, in fact, they would be trained never to bend the sword arm lest the enemy's edged weapon slide off their sabre guard and amputate the elbow. During a charge, enemy fire would be constantly eroding the most forward line of troopers, who, falling, would bring down men of the second row attempting to plug the gaps; the net result of this and the gradual loss of the riders' control over their mounts as they careered forward, would be a disintegration of the strict spacing and uniformly even lines so vital to the success of a charge; in effect, the only manner of maintaining a wall of horseflesh and steel was to cram too many men and horses into far too little space (*Illustration by Job, courtesy of the National Army Museum*)

The cuirassiers' natural leather saddle had dark blue saddle-cloth, portemanteau and holster covers (though these last were rare), all laced in white. In place of the holster covers, the troopers usually employed a half-shabraque of white sheepskin edged with 'wolves' teeth' of the regimental colour. Some idea of the rarity of the use of holster covers or *chaperons* is demonstrated by the fact that, in 1807, the 12th Cuirassiers had only 85 pairs and the 7th Cuirassiers only 65 pairs; in 1808, the 3rd, 4th, 7th, 8th, 9th and 10th regiments are known to have acquired some, but whether they had sufficient numbers and whether these were

ever repaired or replaced as they wore out, is unknown. The saddle-cloth originally had the number of the regiment in white in the angle, but as time passed this was replaced by a white grenade in most cases (that of the 7th Cuirassiers was yellow while those of the 6th and 10th regiments had the regimental number cut out of the body of the grenade). The portemanteau usually bore the regimental number in white at each end, though those of the 6th and 11th Cuirassiers had (*c.* 1810), grenades.

Attached to the top of the portemanteau was the folded cape displaying the serge of the regimental colour uppermost. In an effort to decrease the height of the pack, three black leather straps were added to the saddle, one to the pommel and two about the holsters, by which the rolled cape might be secured; this served a second purpose in that it made the cape more readily accessible in bad weather. The portemanteau was held in place by three white Hungarian leather straps.

Officers of cuirassiers had a dark blue French saddle, edged in blue lace; a cloth girth; red leather stirrup-leathers; bronzed stirrups; black leather martingale, false-martingale, crupper, bridle and reins, and stable-halter; silver parade-halter and reins; silvered buckles; and silver-tipped holsters. The saddle-cloth was dark blue, piped in the regimental colour and edged in silver lace of the following widths: second-lieutenants, 35mm.; lieutenants, 40mm.; captains, 45mm.; and majors, *chefs d'escadrons* and colonels, 50mm. Those of colonels and majors also had a 15mm.-wide secondary strip of lace on the inside of the wider strip. The holster covers were identical but officers tended to prefer a black sheepskin half-shabraque, edged with 'wolves' teeth' of the regimental colour.

For everyday use, the officers employed a dark

Maréchal-des-logis-chef, standard-bearer, of the 7th Cuirassiers, 1813–14. This senior NCO carries the regimental standard of 1812 pattern. Prior to this date, each squadron of cavalry had its own guidon marked with both its and the regiment's number; but this practice led to a good many losses and it was therefore determined that each regiment should have but one eagle. The bearer's rank is indicated by his mixed silver and scarlet epaulettes and the twin strips of silver lace on scarlet ground sewn on each forearm (here invisible). Only four cuirassier standards were lost in the course of the wars: that of the 1st Cuirassiers at Taroutina, 18 October 1812; that of the 14th Cuirassiers at the Berezina, 26–29 November 1812; that of the 4th Cuirassiers on the retreat towards Vilna in 1812; and, finally, that of the 9th Cuirassiers on that same road (Illustration by Benigni, courtesy of the De Gerlache de Gomery Collection)

blue saddle-cloth, with dark blue holster covers, edged in blue goat's hair and without ornament in the angle. Officers were also frequently mounted on English saddles equipped in the same manner as the French; neither variety having a cantle, they were both devoid of portemanteaux.

Before 1810, the carabiniers sat a natural leather French saddle with Hungarian leather stirrup-leathers and portemanteau straps, blackened iron stirrups, black leather martingale, false-martingale, crupper and boot for the musket, and a grey cloth girth. The saddle-cloth was dark blue with white grenade and lace, of which there were two strips after 1808. Again, the holster covers were rarely used as against a white sheepskin half-shabraque with scarlet 'teeth'. Bridle, reins and parade-halter were of black leather, while the stable and feed-halters were of Hungarian leather. The portemanteau was dark blue with white lace and grenade patch.

After 1810, the carabiniers were assigned a French saddle with natural leather holsters, girth, seat and stirrup-leathers; blackened iron stirrups; and black leather crupper, martingale, musket boot and portemanteau straps. The saddle-cloth and portemanteau were light blue with white grenades and strips of lace. The sheepskin shabraque was given teeth of light blue. The 1812 Regulations made only minor modifications in removing the inner, narrow strip of white lace from the saddle-cloth and adding three black leather straps to the pommel and holsters to which the cape could be tied.

Prior to 1810, officers of carabiniers had a dark blue saddle with silver-tipped holsters and bronzed stirrups. The saddle-cloth was piped in red and had silver lace, regulated in width in the same manner as for cuirassier officers, and silver grenade. The holsters had covers either identical with the saddle-cloth or fashioned of bearskin. After 1810, the saddle had Hungarian leather stirrup-leathers and bronzed stirrups. The saddle-cloth became light blue, as did the holster covers. The martingale, false-martingale, headstall and stable-halter were of black leather, while the parade-halter was in silver. The 1812 Regulations amended the above to a light blue saddle, edged in blue silk lace, and added a second strip of 15mm.-wide lace to the saddle-cloths and holster covers, in gold for majors

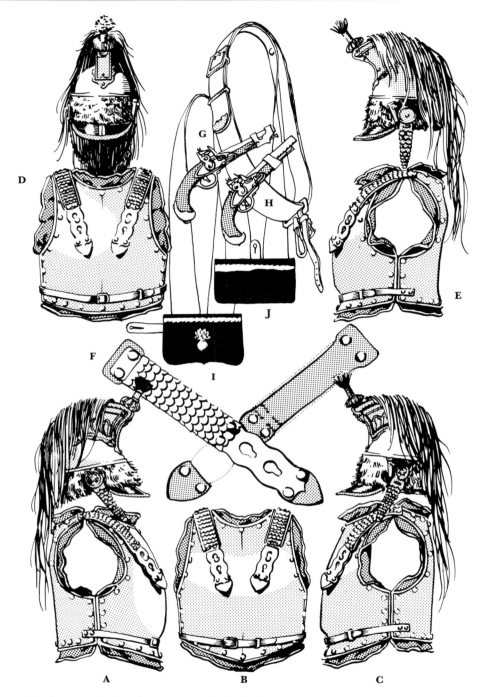

Equipment of cuirassier troopers: *A & B:* The MkI pattern cuirass issued from 1802–5. *C:* The MkII pattern, with which troopers were equipped from 1806–8. *D & E:* The MkIII pattern, in service from 1809–15. *F:* The copper-scaled shoulder strap in detail, from above and below. *G:* The 'AnIX' pattern cavalry pistol with which both cuirassiers and carabiniers were armed. *H:* The 'AnXIII' model cavalry pistol, used in conjunction with the above model again by both carabiniers and cuirassiers. *I:* The 'AnXI' pattern cartridge-pouch and crossbelt complete with horizontal securing strap, by which it would be fastened to a tunic button, and brass grenade badge. *J:* The 1812 Regulations model of cartridge-pouch, crossbelt and musketoon belt and sling. Note the difference in size and shape of this pattern of cartridge-pouch to that carried prior to 1812

and silver for colonels.

For everyday and campaign, officers employed saddle-cloth and portemanteau of light blue with a 40mm.-wide strip of light blue goat's hair about the edge, both devoid of silver grenade devices.

★ ★ ★

It should be borne in mind, however, that neither carabiniers or cuirassiers were as well turned out and homogenous in dress as regulations imply and artists and writers express. In reality, most regiments were in a continual state of chronic disrepair, of which the following report, from Marshal Davout to the Emperor, concerning General Doumerc's inspection of the 4th Cuirassiers on 25 January 1812 at Hamburg, speaks most eloquently:

'Dress . . . I perceived to be very bad, not through lack of good will between officers and men, but by reason of the terrible state which all members of this regiment are in.

'I noticed that the entire regiment had *surtouts* instead of *habit-vestes;* being unaquainted with any order on this subject, I am at a loss as to which is considered uniform dress. What is certain, however, is that two-thirds of cuirassier regiments are dressed in short tunics and that the other third is in *surtouts;* it would be desirable to come to some decision on this matter so that we might, by that means, get a little uniformity into this item of dress. . . . The surtouts are quite good but their cut is terrible.

'Waistcoats – There are only 247 in use, 530 are required. . . .

'Stable jackets – This regiment uses worn-out habits as stable jackets. In truth, the *chef d'escadron* has received news that we were going to perpetually despatch without delay this item of dress for the years 1810 and 1811. . . .

'Hide breeches – All the cuirassiers have a pair but at least half of them are mediocre. . . .

'Boots – The boots are by-and-large in fairly good condition.

'Helmets – This regiment's helmets are in the most pitiful state imaginable; all the turbans need to be replaced; they are atrocious, and much the same can be said for the peaks; a total overhaul of this item is needed, only the caps and the crests are capable of being used. . . .

'Cuirasses – These are generally good, but they need considerable repairs such as having them rebored, which entails great expenditure since the rivets will all have to be removed and then replaced. Further, the waistbelts are too short or worn in some cases and these need replacing; the shoulder-straps are also in need of a lot of attention.

'Sabres – Two-thirds of the sabre scabbards are of iron and two-thirds are of leather, it so pleased some to have their iron scabbards covered in leather. . . .

'Swordbelts – These are in general bad, there are about a quarter which cannot be worn over the shoulder.

'Cartridge-pouches – One thing which surprised me was to see this regiment without cartridge-pouches and without anything in which they might store their cartridges. The *chef d'escadron,* acting commander of the regiment, informed me that these have been lacking since the formation of this corps of cuirassiers. The crossbelts having, he added, been useful for repairing the swordbelts. As to the cartridge-pouch proper, no one knows what these might have been used for.

'Saddles – these are in fairly good condition. . . .

'Shabraques – these are all terribly bad. . . .

The 1804-pattern squadron eagle of the 2nd squadron of the 3rd Cuirassiers. The staff is dark blue with a brass eagle on top. Total height of the staff was 2·1m., while the eagle and socket measured 31cm. and the flag itself, 60cm. by 60cm. This standard would also have been carried by a *maréchal-des-logis-chef*

'Portemanteaux – There are 777 currently in use of which 400 deserve to be taken out of service. . . .

'Capes – Of 776, there are 300 good ones, 376 mediocre ones and 100 which should be destroyed.

'. . . I cannot close this report without informing Your Excellency that fifty men despatched from the depot some ten days since, arrived without other clothing than an old short tunic for use as stable jacket, a pair of hide breeches, gaiters and a pair of shoes. It is inconceivable that anyone should have allowed men to set off so badly protected against the weather of this season.'

The generalisations relating to dress and equipment quoted above therefore provide only a thumb-nail sketch of the *principles* behind the dress of the troops. Inspection reports and contemporary illustrations throw up fascinating anomalies which, along with specific details of the dress of the different ranks, are too lengthy to be quoted here; the reader is referred instead to the illustrations which, we trust, speak for themselves.

There remains only to return to the regiments in order to examine their individual histories and war records. Their number and busy service records regretably oblige us to restrict ourselves to the barest mention of their campaigns and battles, leaving the stirring tales of individual feats of arms for another occasion.

War Service of Individual Regiments

1st Cuirassiers

Regimental history:
1635: Admitted into French service from the Army of the Duke of Saxe-Weimar.
1657: Named Colonel-Général.
1791: Became 1er Régiment de Cavalerie.
1801: Renamed 1er Régiment de Cavalerie-Cuirassiers.
1803: Renamed 1er Régiment de Cuirassiers.
1814: Renamed the Cuirassiers du Roi.
1815: Renumbered as the 1er Régiment de Cuirassiers, only to be disbanded on 16 July at Loches.

War record:
1805: With the Grande Armée at Wertingen, Ulm, Hollabrünn, Raussnitz and Austerlitz.
1806: With the Grande Armée at Jena and Lübeck.
1807: With the Grande Armée at Hoff and Eylau.
1809: Part of the Armée d'Allemagne at Eckmuehl, Ratisbonne, Essling, Wagram, Hollabrünn and Znaïm.
1812: With the Grande Armée at La Moskowa and Winkovo.
1813: With the Grande Armée at the Katzbach, Leipzig, Hanau and the defence of Hamburg.
1814: Fought at La Chaussée, Vauchamps, Bar-sur-Aube, Sézanne and Valcourt.
1815: Fought at Ligny, Genappes and Waterloo.

2nd Cuirassiers

Regimental history:
1635: Created from Cardinal Richelieu's ordnance company and named Cardinal-Duc.
1643: Renamed Royal-Cavalerie.
1791: Became 2eme Régiment de Cavalerie.
1802: Renamed 2eme Régiment de Cavalerie-Cuirassiers.
1803: Renamed 2eme Régiment de Cuirassiers.
1814: Became the Régiment de Cuirassiers de la Reine.
1815: Renamed 2eme Régiment de Cuirassiers and disbanded later the same year.

War record:
1805–7: With the Grande Armée at Wertingen, Austerlitz, Glottau and Friedland.
1809: Part of the Armée d'Allemagne at Eckmuehl, Ratisbonne, Essling and Wagram.
1812: With the Grande Armée at Ostrowno, La Moskowa and Stakov.
1813: With the Grande Armée at Reichenbach, Dresden and Wachau.
1814: Fought at La Rothière, Rosnay, Champaubert, Vauchamps, Athies, La Fère-Champenoise and Paris.
1815: Fought at Quatre-Bras and Waterloo.

3rd Cuirassiers

Regimental history:
1645: Created from three new and three old cavalry companies.
1654: Named Commissaire-Général.
1791: Became 3eme Régiment de Cavalerie.
1802: Renamed 3eme Régiment de Cavalerie-Cuirassiers.

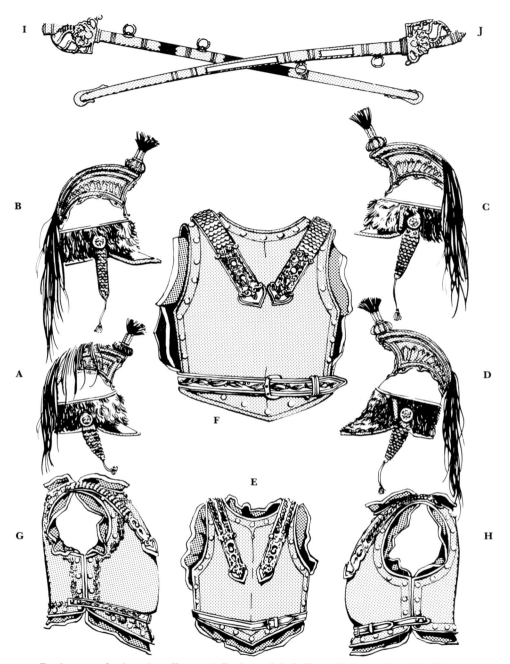

Equipment of cuirassier officers: *A:* Early model of officers' helmet, 1804–6. *B:* Helmet of senior officer of the 11th Cuirassiers, 1807–9. Of interest is the large number of differences between this and the previous model despite their chronological proximity. *C:* Helmet of a superior officer of the 13th Cuirassiers 1809–12. At this point we can perceive the near-fruition of the neo-classical style of officers' helmet: the cap is swept perceptibly higher and farther back, while the crest has become taller and farther forward than on either of the preceding models. *D:* The culmination of the Grecian-influenced helmet style, the 'Minerve', 1810–15. *E:* The officers' version of the MkI troopers' cuirass, 1804–9. *F:* Another version of the above cuirass, curiously missing the engraved line about the bottom. *G:* Cuirass of a superior officer with laurel leaf motif ornament, 1804–9. *H:* The MkIII officers' cuirass, 1809–15. *I:* The straight bladed officers' sabre worn throughout the wars. *J:* The same sabre hilt mounted on a curved 'Montmorency' blade

1803: Renamed 3eme Régiment de Cuirassiers.
1814: Became the Régiment de Cuirassiers du Dauphin.
1815: Renamed 3eme Régiment de Cuirassiers and disbanded on 25 November.

War record:
1805: With the Grande Armée at Austerlitz.
1806–7: With the Grande Armée at Jena, Heilsberg and Friedland.
1809: With the Armée d'Allemagne at Eckmuehl, Essling and Wagram.
1812: Fought at La Moskowa.
1813: Fought at Dresden and Leipzig.
1814: Fought at Champaubert.
1815: Fought at Fleurus and Waterloo.

4th Cuirassiers

Regimental history:
1643: Formed of twelve volunteer companies of cavalry and named La Reine-Mère.
1666: Renamed La Reine.
1791: Became 4eme Régiment de Cavalerie.
1802: Renamed 4eme Régiment de Cavalerie-Cuirassiers.
1803: Renamed 4eme Régiment de Cuirassiers.
1814: Became the Régiment de Cuirassiers d'Angoulême.
1815: Renamed 4eme Régiment de Cuirassiers and disbanded at Fontenay on 21 December.

War record:
1805: With the Armée d'Italie at Caldiero and the crossing of the Tagliamento.
1807: With the Grande Armée at Marienwerder and Heilsberg.
1809: Part of the Armée d'Allemagne at Essling and Wagram.
1812: With the Grande Armée at Polotsk, Smoliany, Borisov and the crossing of the Berezina.
1813: With the Grande Armée at Bautzen, Dresden, Wachau, Leipzig and the siege of Hamburg.
1814: Fought at Brienne, La Rothière, Champaubert, Vauchamps, Laon, La Fère-Champenoise and Paris.
1815: Fought at Ligny and Waterloo.

5th Cuirassiers

Regimental history:
1653: Creation of the regiment.
1725: Named Stanislas-Roi.

1737: Renamed Royal-Pologne.
1791: Became 5eme Régiment de Cavalerie.
1803: Renamed 5eme Régiment de Cuirassiers.
1814: Became the Régiment de Cuirassiers de Berry.
1815: Renamed 5eme Régiment de Cuirassiers and later disbanded.

War record:
1805: With the Grande Armée at Hollabrünn, Brunn and Austerlitz.
1806–7: With the Grande Armée at Jena, Lübeck, Hoff, Eylau, Wittenberg and Königsberg.
1808: The 1st squadron was on service in Spain.
1809: Part of the Armée d'Allemagne at Rohr, Eckmuehl, Ratisbonne, Essling and Wagram.
1812: With the Grande Armée at La Moskowa and Winkovo.
1813: With the Grande Armée at Leipzig and Hanau.
1814: Fought at Montmirail, Bar-sur-Aube, Troyes, Nogent and Saint-Dizier.
1815: Fought at Ligny and Waterloo.

6th Cuirassiers

Regimental history:
1635: Formed and named the Dragons du Cardinal.
1638: Renamed the Fusiliers à Cheval de son Eminence.
1643: Renamed the Fusiliers à Cheval du Roi.
1646: Renamed the Régiment du Roi.
1791: Became 6eme Régiment de Cavalerie.
1803: Renamed 6eme Régiment de Cuirassiers.
1815: Became the Régiment du Colonel-Général on 16 January, renamed 6eme Régiment de Cuirassiers on 20 March and disbanded later the same year.

War record:
1805: With the Armée d'Italie at Verona and Caldiero.
1807: With the Grande Armée at Heilsberg.
1809: With the Armée d'Allemagne at Eckmuehl, Essling and Wagram.
1812: With the Grande Armée at La Moskowa, Winkovo and Malojaroslavetz.
1813: With the Grande Armée at Dresden, Wachau and Leipzig.
1814: Fought at Champaubert.
1815: Fought at Waterloo.

7th Cuirassiers

Regimental history:
1659: Formed and named the Royal-Étranger.

1 Trooper of the 9th Cuirassiers in full
  dress, early 1804
2 Trumpeter of the 9th Cuirassiers in full
  dress, 1804-1805
3 Officer of the 3rd Cuirassiers, 1804–1805

ANGUS McBRIDE

A

1 Trumpeter of the 7th Cuirassiers, 1805–1809
2 Marechal-des-logis of the 2nd Cuirassiers, 1806
3 Superior officer of the 7th Cuirassiers, 1807

B

ANGUS. McBRIDE

1 Trooper of the 5th Cuirassiers, 1807–1809
2 Officer of the 10th Cuirassiers, 1807–1809
3 Officer of the 4th Cuirassiers, 1804–1809

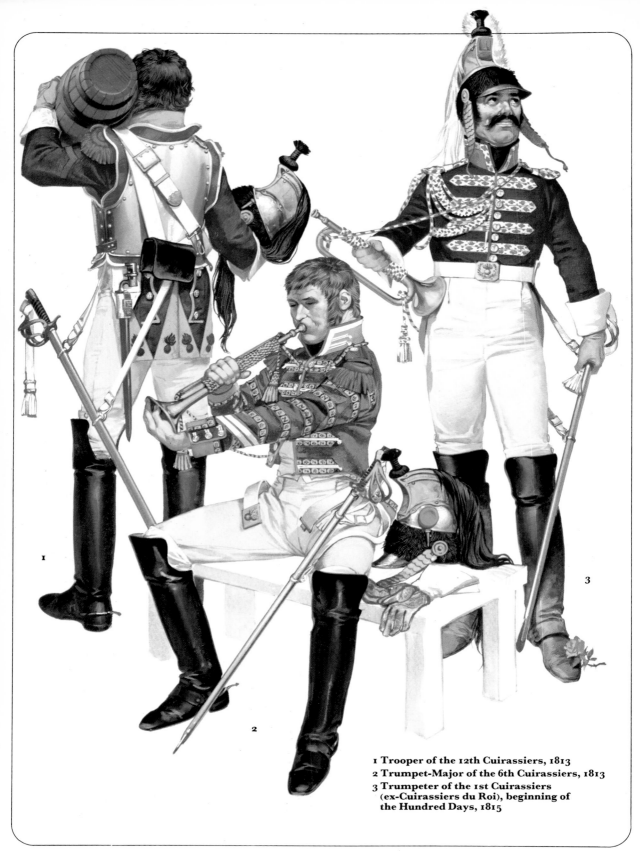

1 Trooper of the 12th Cuirassiers, 1813
2 Trumpet-Major of the 6th Cuirassiers, 1813
3 Trumpeter of the 1st Cuirassiers
(ex-Cuirassiers du Roi), beginning of
the Hundred Days, 1815

D

1 Carabinier in full dress, 1808–1810
2 Officer of the 2nd Carabiniers, 1809
3 Trumpeter of the 2nd Carabiniers in full dress, 1807–1810

ANGUS McBRIDE

E

F

1 Marechal-des-logis of the 1st Carabiniers,
  1808–1810
2 Trumpeter of the 1st Carabiniers, early 1810
3 Officer of carabiniers in full dress, 1807–1810

ANGUS McBRIDE

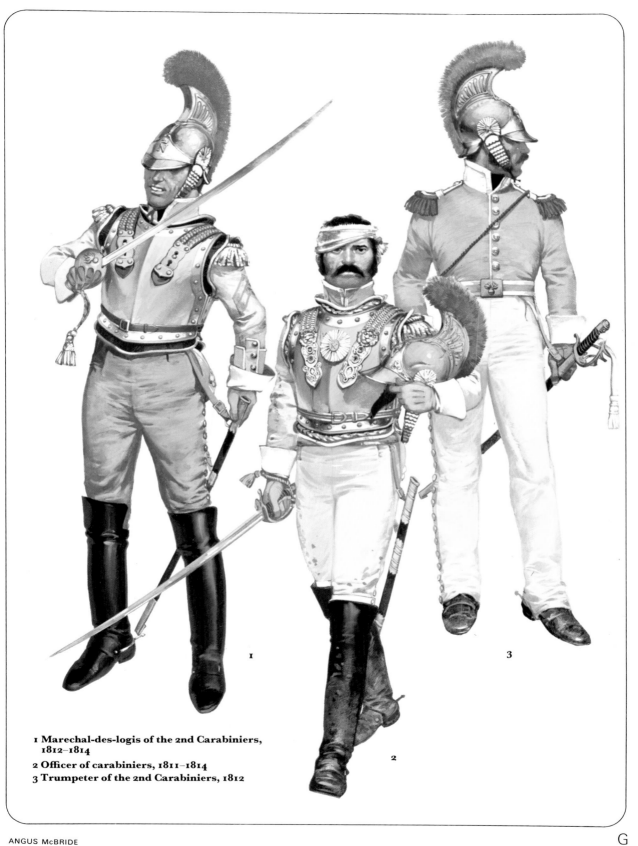

1 **Marechal-des-logis of the 2nd Carabiniers,**
  1812–1814
2 **Officer of carabiniers, 1811–1814**
3 **Trumpeter of the 2nd Carabiniers, 1812**

1 Trooper of the 1st Carabiniers, 1812
2 Officer of carabiniers in overcoat
3 Trumpeter of the 1st Carabiniers, 1813–1815

H

ANGUS McBRIDE

1791: Became 7eme Régiment de Cavalerie.
1803: Renamed 7eme Régiment de Cuirassiers.
1815: Disbanded.

War record:
1805: With the Armée d'Italie at the crossing of the Tagliamento.
1806: Part of d'Espagne's division of the Grande Armée.
1807: With the Grande Armée at Heilsberg.
1809: With the Armée d'Allemagne at Essling and Wagram.
1812: With the Grande Armée, Doumerc's division of Oudinot's corps, at Polotsk and the crossing of the Berezina.
1813: Fought at Reichenbach, Dresden and Leipzig.
1814: Fought at Champaubert and Vauchamps.
1815: Fought at Ligny and Waterloo.

8th Cuirassiers

Regimental history:
1665: Created from the Mestre-de-Camp company of the Régiment de Villequier in 1638, the regiment was now named the Cuirassiers du Roi.
1791: Became 8eme Régiment de Cavalerie.
1803: Renamed 8eme Régiment de Cuirassiers.
1815: Disbanded at Saumur on 5 December.

War record:
1805: With the Armée d'Italie at Caldiero and the crossing of the Tagliamento.
1807: With the Grande Armée at Heilsberg.
1809: With the Armée d'Allemagne at Essling and Wagram.
1812: With the Grande Armée at La Moskowa.
1813: With the Grande Armée at Leipzig and Hanau.
1814: Fought at Vauchamps.
1815: Fought at Quatre-Bras and Waterloo.

9th Cuirassiers

Regimental history:
1684: Formed from the volunteer company of the old Régiment de Villars (created in 1666).
1686: Named the Régiment d'Anjou.
1753: Renamed the Régiment d'Aquitaine.
1761: Renamed the Régiment d'Artois.
1791: Became 9eme Régiment de Cavalerie.
1803: Renamed 9eme Régiment de Cuirassiers.
1815: Disbanded at Poitiers on 16 July.

War record:
1805: With the Grande Armée at Austerlitz.
1806-8: With the Grande Armée at Jena and Friedland.
1809: With the Armée d'Allemagne at Eckmuehl, Ratisbonne and Essling.
1812: With the Grande Armée at Ostrovno, La Moskowa and Winkovo.
1813: With the Grande Armée at Lützen, Bautzen, Dresden and Leipzig.
1814: Fought at Saint-Dizier, Brienne, La Rothière, Champaubert, Vauchamps, Craonne and La Fère-Champenoise.
1815: Fought at Ligny and Waterloo.

10th Cuirassiers

Regimental history:
1643: Created from the remainders of the Croatian regiments in French service which had been disbanded at the time of Louis XIII's death and named the Royal-Cravates.
1791: Became 10eme Régiment de Cavalerie.
1803: Renamed 10eme Régiment de Cuirassiers.
1815: Disbanded at Angers and Fontenay-le-Comte.

War record:
1805: With the Grande Armée at Austerlitz.
1806-7: With the Grande Armée at Jena, Eylau and Hoff.
1809: With the Armée d'Allemagne at Eckmuehl and Wagram.
1812: Fought at La Moskowa.
1813-14: With the Grande Armée at Leipzig and Hamburg.
1815: Fought at Waterloo.

11th Cuirassiers

Regimental history:
1665: Created from the Mestre-de-Camp company of the Régiment de Montclar.
1668: Named the Royal-Roussillon.
1791: Became 11eme Régiment de Cavalerie.
1803: Renamed 11eme Régiment de Cuirassiers.
1815: Disbanded.

War record:
1805: With the Grande Armée at Austerlitz.
1806-7: With the Grande Armée at Eylau and Friedland.
1809: With the Armée d'Allemagne at Ratisbonne and Essling.

Brigadier of the 4th and trooper of the 11th Cuirassiers 1810. These unarmoured cuirassiers are wearing the 1809 *habit-surtout* which was to present serious problems of identification. The reason for this lay in the fact that several regiments would share the same facing colour but were hitherto identifiable by the positioning of the colour and the direction of the tail pockets. The 1809 *habit-surtout*, being devoid of both cuff-slashes and tail pockets, therefore required a re-organisation of the facing colours which, though known to historians, are of uncertain specific origin

1812: With the Grande Armée at La Moskowa, Winkovo and Tholoschinn.
1813: With the Grande Armée at Dresden and Leipzig.
1814: Fought at Laon.
1815: With the Armée du Nord at Ligny and Waterloo.

12th Cuirassiers

Regimental history:
1668: Created from various companies of reformed regiments and one company of the Chevau-Légérs du Dauphin. Named Le Dauphin.
1791: Became 12eme Régiment de Cavalerie.
1803: Renamed 12eme Régiment de Cuirassiers.
1815: Disbanded at Niort.

War record:
1805: With the Grande Armée at Wertingen, Elchingen, Hollabrünn and Austerlitz.
1806-7: With the Grande Armée at Jena, Heilsberg and Friedland.
1809: With the Armée d'Allemagne at Eckmuehl, Ratisbonne, Essling and Wagram.
1812: With Valence's Division of the 1st Reserve Corps of the Grande Armée at Mohilev, La Moskowa and Winkovo.
1813: With Bordesoulle's Division of the Grande Armée at Bautzen, Reichenbach, Jauer, Dresden, Wachau and Leipzig.
1814: Fought at La Rothière, Rosnay, Champaubert, Vauchamps, Valjouan, Athies, Reims, La Fère-Champenoise and Paris.
1815: With Milhaud's 4th Corps of the Reserve Cavalry at Ligny and Waterloo.

13th Cuirassiers

Regimental history:
1807: Formed, in December, at Libourne from detachments of existing regiments of cuirassiers and carabiniers★. Named the 1er Régiment Provisoire de Grosse Cavalerie.
1808: Became 13eme Régiment de Cavalerie having been amalgamated with most of the 2eme Régiment Provisoire de Grosse Cavalerie★★.
1814: Disbanded in July at Colmar.

War record:
1808–13: Fought in Spain at Tudela, the siege of Saragossa, the battle of Saragossa, Villareal, the siege of Lerida, Margalef-Lerida, the siege of Tarragona, Sagonte, Castalla and the Ordal pass.
1814: Fought at Lyon.

★The regiment was composed of men from the 1st and 2nd Carabiniers and the 1st, 2nd and 3rd Cuirassiers.
★★This second provisional regiment consisted of men from the 5th, 9th, 10th, 11th and 12th Cuirassiers who had survived the Baylen catastrophe.

A third provisional regiment was created in 1808 of detachments of the 4th, 6th, 7th and 9th Cuirassiers but was disbanded in 1809.

14th Cuirassiers

1810: The Dutch 2nd Regiment of Cuirassiers were incorporated in the French army and named 14eme Régiment de Cuirassiers.

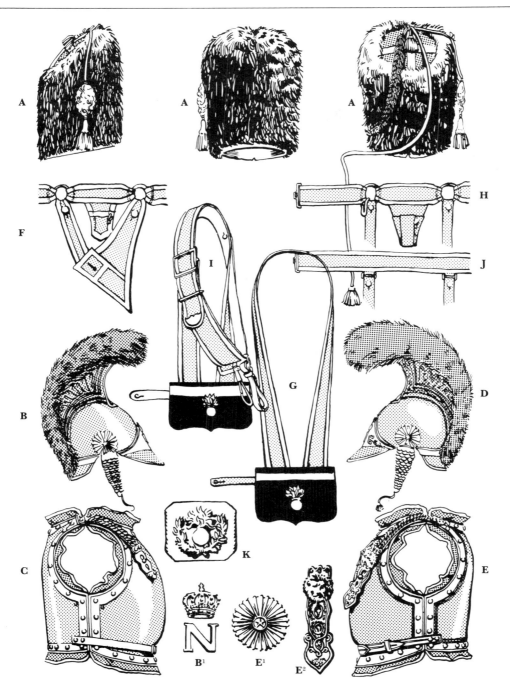

Equipment of carabinier officers and troopers: *A:* The carabiniers' bearskin as described by the 'AnX' Regulations, originally 318mm. but rarely below 350mm. towards 1810. *B & B¹:* Helmet and front decoration as worn by troopers from late 1810. *C:* The troopers'-pattern cuirass. *D:* The officers' model of post 1810 helmet. Note that the crest is rather larger than that of the troopers' version. *E, E¹ and E²:* The officers' model cuirass, sunburst device from its breast and shoulder-strap detail. *F:* The 'AnIX'-pattern troopers' swordbelt. *G:* The troopers' cartridge-pouch prior to 1810. *H:* Troopers' swordbelt and bayonet frog, post 1809. *I:* Troopers' cartridge-pouch and musketoon crossbelt as carried post 1811. *J:* Officers'-pattern swordbelt, worn before and after 1810. *K:* Officers' swordbelt buckle

Unarmoured cuirassiers of (from left to right) the 3rd, 9th and 5th Cuirassiers, 1805. On the left, a cuirassier in town dress: the *surtout* has replaced the *habit-veste* and a chapeau, the helmet; the breeches would be exchanged for a pair in dark blue, worn with dark blue or black stockings, in winter. The centre figure demonstrates the continued use of the old *cavalerie* habits, with their long ungainly skirt, until the arrival of the short-skirted 1803 *habit-surtout*. On the right, a cuirassier in off-duty wear, including the *surtout*, stable trousers, buckled shoes and fatigue-cap; note his queued hair (*Illustration by Benigni, courtesy of the De Gerlache de Gomery Collection*)

1809: With the Armée d'Allemagne at Eckmuehl, Ratisbonne, Essling and Wagram.

1812: With the Grande Armée at La Moskowa, Winkovo and Viasma.

1813: With the Grande Armée at Dresden, Leipzig and Hanau.

1814: Fought at Montmirail, La Guillotière, Troyes, Craonne, Laon and Reims.

1815: Fought at Quatre-Bras and Waterloo.

The Carabinier Regiments

Regimental histories:

1693: Formed of an amalgamation of all seven existing carabinier companies and named the Royal-Carabiniers.

1758: Renamed the Carabiniers de M. le Comte de Provence.

1774: Renamed the Carabiniers de Monsieur.

1791: Become 1er and 2eme Régiments de Carabiniers.

1815: Disbanded and then reformed as the Carabiniers de Monsieur.

War record:

1805: With the Grande Armée at Nuremberg and Austerlitz.

1806–7: With the Grande Armée at Prentzlov, Lübeck, Ostrolenka, Guttstadt and Friedland.

A *chef d'escadron* in ball dress, 1806–10. For full ball dress, the helmet would be replaced by a felt bicorn and the short-skirted habit by a long-tailed, lapelled tunic reminiscent of, and frequently actually, the old *cavalerie* habit. Notice the use of an épée in lieu of the *sabre de bataille* (*Illustration by Benigni, courtesy of the De Gerlache de Gomery Collection*)

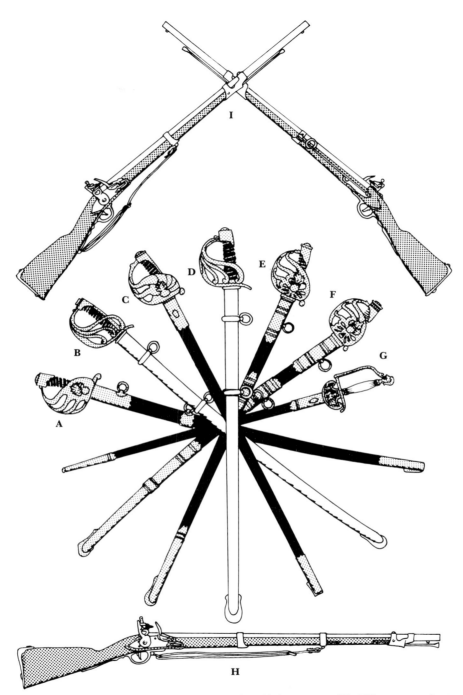

Weapons of cuirassiers and carabiniers: *A:* Carabinier troopers' 'AnIX'-pattern sabre. *B:* Iron scabbarded carabinier troopers' sabre post 1810. *C:* Carabinier troopers' 'AnIV'-pattern sabre. *D:* Cuirassier troopers' 'AnXI'-pattern sabre. *E:* The 'AnIV'-pattern carabinier officers'-pattern sabre. *F:* Carabinier officers' sabre with the 'AnIV' hilt remounted on a Montmorency blade. *G:* Typical épée carried by officers of carabiniers and cuirassiers in walking-out dress. *H:* The short, 1·20m., artillery model 'AnIX'-pattern musket carried by troopers of carabiniers prior to 1810. *I:* The 'AnIX'-pattern cavalry musketoon used by troopers of cuirassiers and carabiniers after 1811

Cuirassiers in capes, 1813. Before 1813, a long, sack-like cloak was issued for use in bad weather, as worn by the left-hand figure. The 1812 Regulations altered this garment to include sleeves, thereby making it more of a greatcoat than a cape, as worn by the figure on the right. Unlike that carried by dragoons, the post-1812 cuirassier cape was seemingly without buttons on the body or shoulder cape with which it might be secured closed (*Illustration by Benigni, courtesy of the De Gerlache de Gomery Collection*)

The Plates

A1   Trooper of the 9th Cuirassiers in full dress, early 1804.

This cuirassier wears the first full dress uniform of the new cuirassier heavy cavalry arm. Beneath the armour, a single-breasted tunic with short skirt now replaced the old *cavalerie habit-veste*. Although a letter from the Ministry of War, dated 20 December 1803, to this regiment specified that the new tunic was to have shoulder-straps and no ornaments on the turnbacks, it is likely that the 9th regiment opted for the scarlet epaulettes and dark blue grenade insignia by 1805. Similarly, the official black plume topped with the regimental colour would be swapped for a red one. Of interest is this fellow's powdered and queued hair,

a hallmark of all those regiments which formed a part of Nansouty's Division as late as 1809.

A2   Trumpeter of the 9th Cuirassiers in full dress, 1804–1805.

This reconstruction of the trumpeter's uniform from official regulations would at first appear to contradict other references, notably the Marckolsheim MS, which indicate that a pink tunic was carried at this period. In fact, the oft-quoted pink garment's origin lies in the Consulate's Decree of 31 December 1802 which, in eliminating those regiments of *cavalerie* numbered 19 through 22, incorporated fresh troops into regiments 9 through 18 to bring them up to strength; the 9th regiment thereby received a company of both the 19th and 22nd regiments whose troops retained the uniforms of their old regiments of which the distinctive colour was pink. From 1805, the colours of the tunic was reversed, that is dark blue facings on a yellow tunic, until the advent of the dark green Imperial Livery issued from 1811.

A3   Officer of the 3rd Cuirassiers, 1804–1805

Officers' no. 2 riding dress consisted of the *surtout*, a single-breasted long skirted jacket, worn with a white waistcoat of linen or cashmere and riding breeches. These last were generally white for summer wear and dark blue for winter. Equipment was as that for full dress with the exception of the slimmer swordknot and the option of wearing helmet or bicorn. Note also that short gloves replace the cuffed variety. In these early years, the *cavalerie* tunic was frequently worn for walking-out dress, but, in this particular instance, the Colonel of the regiment specified that the *surtout* tunic as shown here was to be worn for both riding and society dress.

B1   Trumpeter of the 7th Cuirassiers, 1805–1809

This full dress figure illustrates one of several variations in uniform at this period. While an inspection report dated October 1805 maintains that there were as many cuirasses as men, including trumpeters, in this regiment, only one source, the Marckolsheim MS, shows a trumpeter so armoured. Martinet and Valmont insist on the other hand that no cuirass was worn. In their depictions of the tunic, they complicate the issue still further, for,

Officer of the 3rd Cuirassiers 1805 and officer of the 10th Cuirassiers, 1806. They wear the double-breasted overcoat popular with officers both before and after 1812. This garment, in conjunction with a fatigue-cap, was used for both morning and undress wear on foot (*Illustration by Benigni, courtesy of the De Gerlache de Gomery Collection*)

Officers of the 4th and 5th Cuirassiers, 1813. These officers wear the undress *surtout*, as prescribed by the 1812 Regulations, for full dress on foot. Note the use of short gloves in place of the cuffed variety employed for riding (*Illustration by Goichon, courtesy of the De Gerlache de Gomery Collection*)

while the basic yellow colouring of the garment is not disputed, they disagree as to whether the lace was white or light blue and the turnbacks yellow, white or dark blue. Perhaps it might be best to let the Marckolsheim MS have the last word on the matter; it insists on white lace, and, for good measure, throws in that the epaulettes were scarlet.

B2   Maréchal-des-logis of the 2nd Cuirassiers, 1806
As of 1806, all new cuirassier tunics were made with the addition of old-style lapels of the regimental colour, but this NCO, his grade indicated by the single silver stripe on scarlet ground on each sleeve, still wears the *habit-surtout* with the popular though unofficial fringed epaulettes. Further, despite the fact that the 2nd Cuirassiers were supposedly issued cuirasses of French manufacture in 1803, this individual has the dubious distinction of having received a captured Prussian cuirass

which, though handsome, consisted only of a breastplate. The single silver chevron on his left sleeve denotes his completion of between eight and ten years of military service, while the absence of the tall scarlet plume on his helmet and his wearing button-up overalls indicate that he is on active service. Although here invisible, his hair would be queued.

B3   Superior officer of the 7th Cuirassiers, 1807
This rather elegant figure in campaign dress has heavy silver bullion epaulettes and a richly ornamented cuirass as symbols of rank. Officers' cuirasses were normally only decorated with a deeply engraved single line about 3cm. from the edge and 32 gilded copper rivets on both breast and backplate. The shoulder-straps were made of leather covered in red cloth and had a strip of silver lace down the sides; their ornament at first consisted of

gilded copper scales, but these were eventually replaced by two or three lengths of gilded chain. The waistbelt of the cuirass was of red leather with silver lace and embroidery and a golden buckle. Of interest is the fact that this officer still wears what appears to be, judging from the length of the skirt, the old *cavalerie* tunic which would have had yellow lapels. It would seem that officers had retained these old tunics for off-duty wear and, when the troopers again adopted a lapelled *habit-veste* in 1806, had reintroduced them for service dress.

C1   Trooper of the 5th Cuirassiers, 1807–1809
In anticipation of the rigours of the road ahead, this trooper has thoughtfully encased the plume of his helmet in oilskin and adopted hard-wearing button-up overalls in place of his hide breeches. An inspection report dated 27 July 1805 reveals that this regiment alone persisted in having their *habit-surtouts* manufactured with lapels identical to those reintroduced for all regiments in 1806. A

tenuous connection might perhaps be made between this and the fact that this regiment was the last to receive its cuirasses at the late date of early 1805. The iron cuirass had 34 copper rivets on both breast and backplate, excluding the two which held each end of the waistbelt to the backplate; the shoulder-straps were of leather, sheathed in scarlet fabric and embellished with copper scales.

C2   Officer of the 10th Cuirassiers, 1807–1809
This officer wears the standard uniform of the commissioned ranks for the greater part of the Empire period, with the exception of his interesting cuirass. The officers' pattern breastplate, summarized briefly under B3 above, had an engraved line around the perimeter forming a margin into which rivets were struck, whereas in this instance the line is clearly absent. Further, the waistbelt is of plain black leather instead of the red leather decorated with silver embroidery which one might expect. We can only conclude either that the source – Weiland – is inaccurate; or that for lack

Officer and men of the 3rd Cuirassiers, 1804–5. These figures are dressed for riding instruction, that is in stable dress with the use of riding boots in place of clogs, and overalls in lieu of trousers. Note that the troopers' harness consists only of stable-halter and stirrup-less saddle (*Illustration by Benigni, courtesy of the De Gerlache de Gomery Collection*)

Officer in undress uniform of the 3rd Cuirassiers, 1804–5. In undress, the officers' saddlery consisted solely of a natural leather English or French saddle with dark blue saddle-cloth edged with a 40mm.-wide band of blue goat's hair (*Illustration by Benigni, courtesy of the De Gerlache de Gomery Collection*)

of officers' armour this gentleman has pressed that of a trooper into service – surely the more likely explanation. If this were the case it is entirely feasible that the 'salvageable' parts of the old armour would be added to the new, thus the officers' pattern shoulder-straps and officers' pattern lining with silver lace.

C3   Officer of the 4th Cuirassiers, 1804–1809
This unarmoured officer permits us to examine the *habit-veste* in more detail. This single-breasted tunic, fastened by between seven and ten silver buttons, was the forerunner of the *habit-veste* of 1812 in that it fitted to the waist and had a short skirt. The grenade devices on the turnbacks were embroidered with silver thread and the epaulette loops were also silver. Around 1808, the cut was modified somewhat: the waist tended to be cut higher and the turnbacks were frequently extended all the way round the front of the tunic, ending about an inch wide and joining up with the narrow strip of piping down the front.

In 1809, a new *habit-surtout* was issued to the cuirassiers but, although officers were required to equip themselves with one for wearing with the cuirass, it seems likely that they retained the more practical 1803 tunic for riding, leaving the *habit-surtout* for walking-out and no. 2 dress. With the introduction of the 1812 Regulations, the situation was clarified: officers were attired in a waist-length, lapelled and short-skirted tunic differing from that of the rank and file only in its ornamentation and quality.

D1   Trooper of the 12th Cuirassiers, 1813
After 1812, several changes were made in the equipment of cuirassiers. Having been issued a musketoon and bayonet in early 1812, they now also carried a second crossbelt over the left shoulder, from which the firearm was suspended, and a bayonet frog stitched to the centre section of the swordbelt. The cuirass was of the third pattern, issued from 1809, rounder and shorter, but otherwise identical with previous models.

The helmet, distributed as of 1811, was also of a new pattern, much simplified and most unpopular: the band of copper normally edging the peak was absent, causing the peak to warp out of shape once wet; the crest was devoid of the extrava-

Trumpeter of the 13th Cuirassiers, 1808–9. This trumpeter wears the familiar reversed-colour habit of musicians, in this case *lie de vin* with dark blue facings. The epaulettes are white, as is his helmet's mane (*Illustration by Benigni, courtesy of the De Gerlache De Gomery Collection*)

gant decorations which had hitherto given it great strength, and the absence of a plate of copper on the very top did little to increase its solidity; for lack of this last, water tended to seep into the crest and rot the roots of the horsehair mane which was itself of dubious quality; finally, the copper and iron utilised in the construction of the helmet were of inferior grades. Such was the dislike of this headgear that many cuirassiers departed for Russia in their old helmets, repaired and patched up as well as possible, rather than trust to the new pattern. In 1814, General Saint-Germain opined that the helmet was so defective that nearly all those at that time in service were in dire need of replacement.

D2   Trumpet-Major of the 6th Cuirassiers, 1813
This uniform is a reconstruction of the full dress

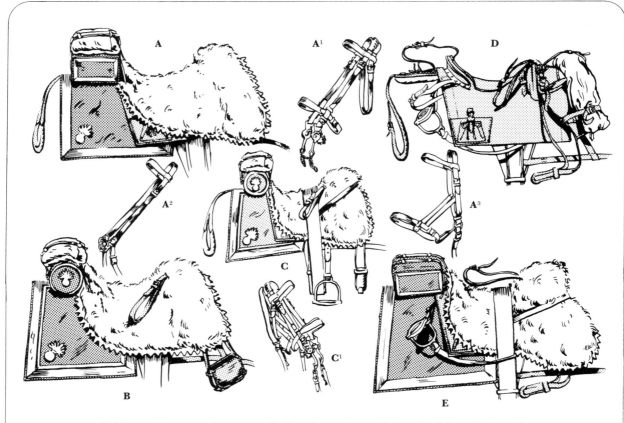

Saddles and harness of troopers of cuirassiers and carabiniers: *A*: Cuirassiers' saddle before 1812. The regimental number would be entered on the ends of the portemanteau in white. *A¹*; *A²* & *A³*: Headstall of the bridle, stable halter and parade halter of cuirassiers. *B*: Carabiniers' saddle before 1810. *C*: The carabiniers' saddle after 1810. *C¹*: Carabiniers bridle, post 1810. *D*: Basic saddle, after Bardin, 1812. *E*: The same saddle but dressed for cuirassiers after the 1812 Regulations

specifications of the 1812 Regulations. The Imperial Livery was an attempt to rationalise the dress of musicians throughout the Grande Armée; hitherto left to the discretion of the colonels, their costume had become so excessive and multi-coloured as the regiments vied with one another for the most striking heads of column, that the situation bordered on chaos.

The new green tunic had facings and piping of the regimental colour, green grenade devices on the turnbacks, white metal buttons and a specially developed lace. This lace, which edged the collar, cuffs, turnbacks, false back pockets, five of the nine buttons down the front and the two in the small of the back, came in two varieties: the one for vertical and the other for horizonal positioning. The design consisted of alternating Imperial 'Ns' and eagles, in green on a yellow base, separated by black thread. Needless to say, official prescriptions were ignored and specimens survive with Imperial 'Ns' in yellow on a green ground, dark green but crowned 'Ns' on a yellow ground, and Imperial eagles facing right or left, with due human disregard for orderly precedent. A 5mm. width of white lace was supposed to be sewn between the double strips of Imperial lace on the button-holes of the cuff-flaps and on the two hooks and eyes of the collar, ending in tiny white tassels as a finishing touch to all this embellishment; there is, however, no trace of this elusive white lace in evidence.

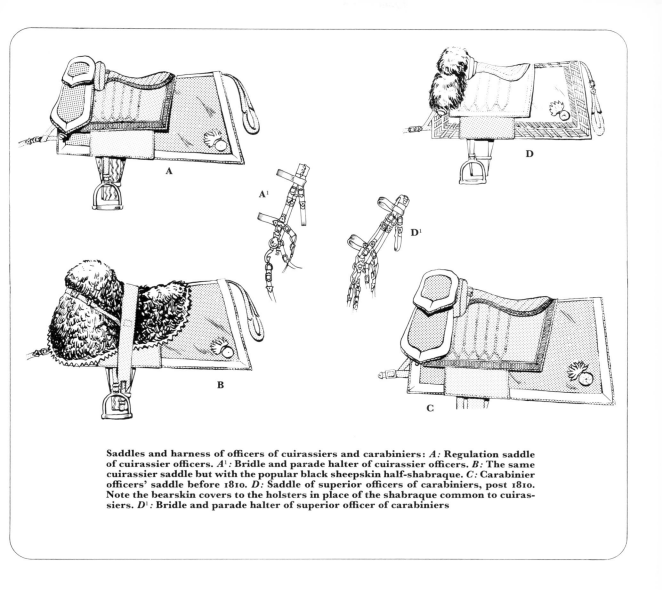

Saddles and harness of officers of cuirassiers and carabiniers: *A*: Regulation saddle of cuirassier officers. *A¹*: Bridle and parade halter of cuirassier officers. *B*: The same cuirassier saddle but with the popular black sheepskin half-shabraque. *C*: Carabinier officers' saddle before 1810. *D*: Saddle of superior officers of carabiniers, post 1810. Note the bearskin covers to the holsters in place of the shabraque common to cuirassiers. *D¹*: Bridle and parade halter of superior officer of carabiniers

The rank of this *brigadier* (corporal) is indicated by the twin strips of white lace on scarlet ground visible on each forearm. Note also the replacement of the plume by an *aurore* lentil-shaped pompon which denotes that he is a member of the first company of the third squadron of this regiment.

D3   Trumpeter of the 1st Cuirassiers (ex-Cuirassiers du Roi), beginning of the Hundred Days, 1815
With the abdication of the Emperor in 1814, all traces of his reign were suppressed and, where possible, eradicated. The Imperial Livery was replaced with this dark blue tunic, bearing the white and crimson lace of the Bourbon dynasty and buttons stamped with the royal fleur-de-lys. Upon

the return of Napoleon for the brief Belgian campaign, not all souvenirs of France's fleeing monarchy could be erased in time for the coming campaign: and this fellow, assuming his survival, would have found himself mercifully well dressed for the reappearance of the deposed Louis XVIII later in the year.

E1   Carabinier in full dress, 1808–1810
The two carabinier regiments were indistinguishable except for the colour of the cuff-flaps: red with blue piping for the 1st Carabiniers and the reverse for the 2nd. The tunic was essentially identical to that prescribed in 1791 bar the grenade devices on the turnbacks which, now white, were

Trumpeter of the 4th Cuirassiers, 1805–9. He wears a single-breasted scarlet habit with white lace loops, a common practice. His epaulettes and horsehair mane are white, and his plume and trumpet cords are scarlet. Trumpeters always rode greys and employed a black sheepskin shabraque in place of the troopers' white ones (Illustration by Benigni, courtesy of the De Gerlache de Gomery Collection)

dark blue prior to 1808. The distinctive bearskin headdress of these two regiments was, according to regulations dated 21 October 1801, 318mm. tall, but became markedly taller as the years passed, certainly never less than 350mm., such being the vanity of man. This headgear had no jugulars but was maintained in place by a leather strap, which passed under the queue of the hair, and a white cord which descended from the top of the bearskin, passed under the left epaulette and was looped about a tunic button. Interestingly, when, in early 1809, the carabiniers were required to wear their hair short, no steps were taken to issue them chinstraps and many men were consequently wounded or killed owing to being hit on the skull, their bearskins trailing behind them and tangling them up in the cord; by the time of the battle of

Wagram, however, the troops were equipped with either copper or white metal scaled chinstraps.

E2   Officer of the 2nd Carabiniers, 1809
This officer in marching order, his plume packed along with his fine white breeches in his porte-manteau, has had armoured jugulars fitted to his headdress. His uniform differs from that of the rank and file only in its finer quality cloth and its silver ornaments in place of white. Officers carried only a sabre as armament (excluding the twin pistols holstered at the front of the saddle), of identical shape to that of the men but sheathed in a more extravagantly fitted scabbard.

E3   Trumpeter of the 2nd Carabiniers in full dress, 1807–1810
Trumpeters wore a tunic of reversed colours with the addition of white lace to the facings. Prior to 1808 the grenade devices were red, but these subsequently became white in line with those of the troopers. A trumpeter of the 1st regiment would be dressed in exactly the same manner but with dark blue epaulettes, edged in white lace, in place of white. Like the officers, trumpeters were armed only with a sabre, but in their case it would be identical with that of the troopers. Before 1807, the plume would have been entirely red. The horse furniture would be the same in all respects as that of the troopers save for a black sheepskin shabraque in place of white. Trumpeters rode greys.

F1   Maréchal-des-logis of the 1st Carabiniers, 1808–1810
This *sous-officier*, his rank indicated by the single silver stripe on each forearm and the mixed silver and red threads of his epaulettes and swordknot, wears the popular *surtout* tunic in lieu of the more formal, and consequently less frequently used, habit. A report to the Emperor dated 5 July 1808 gives us the following insight into the use of the two tunics: '. . . *the carabiniers have owned surtouts for the last three years, the uniform habit has been worn but once. . . .*'. The garment was fastened by between six and eight pewter buttons. Note that the service chevron on the left upper-arm was silver on a red ground for *sous-officiers* as against red for other ranks.

F2   Trumpeter of the 1st Carabiniers, early 1810
With the approaching change-over to armour, the old-fashioned lapelled habit fell still further into disuse in favour of the *surtout*, itself soon to be replaced with a similar but shorter skirted habit. In this instance, the trumpeter's tunic has been decorated with loops of white lace, terminating in tassels, passing about the ventral buttons and anchored to two extra rows of buttons on each breast. This embellishment lasted throughout 1810, even to its use on a short-skirted red tunic, until the arrival of the light blue habits. At one point during the period of adaptation, this same tunic with the addition of lace to the turnbacks

Trumpeter of the 7th Cuirassiers, 1813. After 1812, musicians of all troops of the line were required to wear the Imperial Livery of dark green, an attempt to rationalise the chaotic situation created by leaving the uniforms of the heads of column to the vagaries of the individual regiments' colonels. Although this trumpeter's livery lace has a 5mm.-strip of tasselled white lace between its loops, as prescribed by the Regulations of May 1810, no trace of this exists on garments or on tailors' returns of 1812 or 1813 and it is likely that, in the same manner as the trumpet banners described in the 1812 Regulations, it was never manufactured or issued (*Illustration by Benigni, courtesy of the De Gerlache de Gomery Collection*)

was employed in conjunction with a cuirass. It seems that the regiments were attempting to use up all their existing stocks of red fabric while acquiring those items of equipment of the new uniform as and when they arrived; the short-skirted version of this tunic, mentioned above, was worn with the new white-crested trumpeters' helmet.

F3   Officer of carabiniers in full dress, 1807–1810
Full dress for officers consisted of habit, waistcoat, deer hide breeches, stiff or soft leather boots complete with bronzed spurs, buff swordbelt with gilded copper buckles, cuffed gauntlets and bearskin embellished with full cords and plume. The sabre could be either straight or lightly curved with red or gilded copper hilt; the leather scabbard had gilded copper fittings. Officers utilised a *surtout* as frequently as the men, of identical pattern but of finer materials and with silver decorations. In walking-out dress either of the tunics could be employed, with linen breeches and white stockings in summer, or dark blue or black breeches and black woollen stockings in winter. The outfit was completed by black shoes with silver buckles and a bicorn chapeau with silver tassels in the angles.

G1   Maréchal-des-logis of the 2nd Carabiniers, 1812–1814
The carabiniers suffered such considerable losses during the 1809 campaign that, on 24 December, the Emperor decreed that they were to be armoured in such a manner as to afford them the same protection as the cuirassiers while at the same time maintaining a distinct visual difference between the two types of élite heavy cavalry. To this end, Napoleon selected a yellow copper helmet and an iron cuirass covered in a thin sheet of brass. Although the Emperor desired the tunic to be madder red, he was overruled by the war office which, probably for reasons of economy, opted for a white tunic with sky blue facings. This *sous-officer* wears such a tunic: the sky blue cuff-flaps piped in white distinguished the second regiment from the first; the silver chevrons and single stripe on sky blue ground, and the mixed silver and scarlet epaullettes denoted his rank. He wears a pair of button-up *surculottes* to protect his breeches. Note the mixed silver and scarlet swordknot on his

Trumpeter of the 9th Cuirassiers, 1814. This illustration permits us to examine the rear of the Imperial Livery. Although decreed 23 May 1810, described in the Journal Militaire of 30 December 1811 and detailed in the 1812 Regulations, the livery can only be sure to have been issued from early 1813 (Illustration by Rousselot, courtesy of the De Gerlache de Gomery Collection)

copper-hilted sabre, a further indication of his near-officer status.

G2 Officer of carabiniers, 1811–1814

Officers wore a tunic identical with that of the men but of finer quality and with silver ornaments and buttons. Armour was essentially of the same pattern, but with red copper replacing the yellow copper of the rank and file, and silver replacing the iron. The cuirass was embellished with a silver sun symbol with a gilt star at its centre and had sky blue shoulder-straps edged in silver and ornamented with three silver chains. The dark blue padding of the cuirass was decorated with two strips of silver lace for junior officers and a single strip and laurel leaf border for senior officers. Officers' sabres had hilts of yellow, gilded or red copper, and black leather scabbards with gilded fittings. The swordbelt was ochre edged in silver with a gilded buckle bearing a silver grenade and laurel leaf motif.

G3 Trumpeter of the 2nd Carabiniers, 1812

Trumpeters were dressed in precisely the same manner as the men, bar the usual practice of reversing the colours. This trumpeter, drawn from the Marckolsheim MS, has several unusual features: while trumpeters were supposed to wear a trooper's helmet, it appears that musicians of the 2nd Carabiniers affected a sky blue crest, and those of the 1st Carabiniers a white one. The tunic has been duly reversed, leaving the turnbacks and collar white and prompting a query as to the point of then lacing the collar in white when this would be far from readily visible. Lastly, again on the point of facing colour, another musician of this same regiment is shown as having sky blue cuffs and cuff-flaps, edged with white, contrary to the reversed colour principle and highlighting the white collar/white lace question. As can be seen, trumpeters were equipped with neither cuirass nor cartridge-pouch. The lack of cuirass led to frequent instances of the musicians' tunics being decorated with white lace about the buttons of the breast.

H1 Trooper of the 1st Carabiniers, 1812

The iron cuirass, ornamented with copper rivets, had a skin of brass overall, bar a 25mm. margin which revealed the iron base. The waistbelt was brown leather with a copper buckle, while the shoulder-straps were plain leather (unlike those of the cuirassiers) and covered with two copper chains. The black leather cartridge-pouch was suspended on a white-edged, ochre shoulder-belt worn over the left shoulder over which was hung the musketoon crossbelt which was of the same colouring and construction but marginally wider, ending in a steel clip from which the firearm was hung. The yellow buff waistbelt was composed of three sections linked by copper rings. The middle section had a bayonet frog sewn-to it. The slings were of ochre buff with copper buckles and were attached to the two rings of the iron scabbard.

H2 Officer of carabiniers in overcoat

This cape was the standard officers' issue after 1811, although versions without sleeves were not uncommon. The 1812 Regulations specified that the silver lace was to be dropped from the short cape about the shoulders, but it seems unlikely that this order was ever implemented. The troop-

ers' version was a three quarter-length coat of white cloth (with just a touch of blue thread) until 1813. As of that date, a new overcoat called the *manteau-capote* came into use; it had sleeves, but, unlike the preceding model, was devoid of the sky blue lining cloth on each side of the interiors of the front and back vents.

H3   Trumpeter of the 1st Carabiniers, 1813–1815
This trumpeter is dressed as prescribed by the 1810

A trooper of the 7th Cuirassiers, 1812. This cuirassier wears, during the Russian campaign, the final uniform of the arm which was to carry them through 1815. We must assume that this individual dates to the very beginning of the campaign since, as we have seen, his horse would be unlikely to look anything like so fit after a few months on the march. The saddle has an unbleached fodder bag tied to it in which feed would be stored. Note the boots wrapped in fur to protect the feet from frostbite (*Illustration by Benigni, courtesy of the De Gerlache de Gomery Collection*)

Cuirassiers after the restoration of Louis XVIII. During the First Restoration, the dress of cuirassiers remained precisely that of the 1812 Regulations, save that all Imperial emblems were deleted in favour of the fleur-de-lys. With the return of Louis XVIII after the Hundred Days began a very testy period for the army, with the suppression of all things Imperial – from the changing of the regiments' names to the altering of their uniforms (these were to undergo no less than five major changes in ten years). The resentment caused by the monarchy's denial of recent glories went deep, and grew and festered through the whole of the French people until the Empire was recalled as a 'golden age' with which the current monarchy compared badly (*Illustration by Job, courtesy of the National Army Museum*)

Regulations: a tunic of Imperial Livery pattern, with sky blue facings bar the cuffs of scarlet (to distinguish the regiment from the 2nd Carabiniers who had sky blue cuffs); a trooper's helmet; breeches; boots; and a sabre. Although the Decree establishing the Imperial Livery is dated 23 May 1810, it would appear that no musicians actually acquired the uniform before 1813. As to the dark green trumpet banners described by the 1812 Regulations with their yellow fringes and embroidery, it is certain that they were never manufactured.

SOURCES

Anon., *Manoeuvres de la Cavalerie*.
H. Bouchot, *L'Épopée du costume militaire française*.
Commandant Bucquoy (ed.), *Les uniformes du 1er Empire*.
French Ministry of War, *Historique des corps de troupe française*.
Dr. Hourtouille (ed.), *Soldats et uniformes du 1er Empire*.
Job, *Tenue des troupes de France*.
Marx, *Tableaux synoptiques des manoeuvres de Cavalerie*.
J. Regnault, *Les aigles perdus*.
Col. H. C. B. Rogers, *Napoleon's Army*.
L. Rousselot, *L'Armée Française*.
Various issues of *Tradition*, *La Giberne* and *Le Passepoil*.